12 FACTS ABOUT PROTECTIONISM
AND THE GLOBAL ECONOMY

By

Sa'idu Sulaiman

Email: saisulaiman@yahoo.com

Copyright © 2017 by Sa'idu Sulaiman

All rights reserved. No part of this publication may be reproduced, stored in a retrieval system, or transmitted in any form or by any means, electronic, mechanical, photocopying, recording, or otherwise without the prior written permission of the author.

Published in 2017

by CreateSpace, U.S.A.

ISBN-13:978-1544739038, ISBN 10: 1544739036

CONTENTS

About the Author 1
Preface 3

CHAPTER 1
THE DYNAMISM OF ECONOMIC THOUGHT 4

CHAPTER 2
PROTECTIONISM AS AN ELEMENT OF MERCANTILISM 15
Benefits of Mercantilism 19
Criticisms against Mercantilism 20
Conclusion 24

CHAPTER 3
ANATOMY OF THE GLOBAL ECONOMY IN THE ERA OF ADVANCED GLOBALIZATION 25
The Definition and Features of Globalization 25
The Anatomy the Global Economy 29
The Need for Globoeconomics: the Third Level of Economic Analysis 35
An Illustration of the Anatomy of the Global Economy 40

CHAPTER 4
LESSONS FROM THE AMERICAN EXPERIENCE 47
Trump's Protectionist Policies 48
Repercussions of the Trump's Protectionist Policies 57
Reactions to the Trump's Protectionist Policies 61
Lessons from the American Experience 74

CHAPTER 5
FACTS ABOUT PROTECTIONISM AND THE
GLOBAL ECONOMY
The 12 Facts
Recommendations

About the Author

Sa'idu Sulaiman has been teaching History of Economic Thought for two decades to students of Economics in a tertiary institution in Nigeria. He has written a number of books on different academic disciplines. They include, among others, *The Making of Economics;* his travelogue, *Unforgettable Experiences in Abuja, Manchester and London;* and his recent novels: *The Desperate Migrant,* which reflects the current migration crisis in Europe, and *What Matters Most,* which focuses on the ideal way of life.

PREFACE

This book portrays protectionism as a significant component of mercantilism, a self-centred and antagonistic economic system practiced in Europe from 16th to 18th century. It examines the anatomy of the global economy in the context of globalization which renders protectionism and other macro-economic policies of nations ineffective today. The book also draws lessons from the recent American experiences with protectionist policies of President Donald Trump and concludes its thesis with the statement of 12 facts about protectionism and the global economy. One of them is that the interests of nations running the global economy would naturally and inevitably clash just as the interest of the buyer of a commodity aiming for a low price clashes with that of its seller aiming for a high price. However, this clash does not preclude the transaction; moreover, it does not render the contending parties enemies.

The first chapter briefly reviews the evolution of economics to show the dynamic nature of economic thought. The second chapter looks at the prominent role of protectionism in the mercantilist economic theory and restates the benefits of mercantilism and the criticisms labeled against it by some scholars. The chapter is followed by definition and features of globalization, the anatomy of the global economy and the necessity for adopting globoeconomics as the third level of economic analysis. Chapter Four reviews the reactions to the Trump's protectionist policies by the international community and various sections of the American community and draws some lessons from them.

The last chapter concludes the books with statements of 12 facts about protectionism and the global economy and provides some recommendations, which when considered, will boost the global economy, promote peace and understanding among nations and make the world a safer place of abode.

CHAPTER ONE

THE DYNAMISM OF ECONOMIC THOUGHT

At every point in time man has been conceiving ideas on how to solve economic problems or to face challenges created by the circumstances in which he finds himself. With the acquisition of knowledge, man begins to formulate theories to explain an economic phenomenon and also to employ tools of investigation and analysis in order to explain, predict or control it. Economics as a discipline was not created at given point in time or invented by one individual. It evolved over a period of time through contributions made by several people. No one can state the precise time when people began to study economics or write theories and ideas about it. Bert F. Hoselitz observes that

> Though comprehensive treatment of economics did not appear before the late eighteenth century, economic problems were the subject of literary efforts long before that time. [1]

---

[1] Bert F. Hoselitz (1967, p 242) *A Reader's Guide to the Social Sciences* New York: The Free Press.
http://cepa.newshool.edu/het/profiles/ricardo.htm visited on 25th May 2004.

Before the advent of mercantilism, the most significant economic work in Europe came from the medieval scholastic theorists whose goal was to find an economic system compatible with Christian doctrines of piety and justice.[2] The major theories on how the economy of a nation could be run were developed in the 15th century which marked the beginning of the mercantilist period. Mercantilism was closely associated with trade and commercial activities of an economy.

The mercantilist thought was developed in Western Europe as a result of enlightenment and reasoning brought by renaissance coupled with the rise of Protestantism which weakened blind obedience and strengthened reasoned arguments. The mercantilists, who should not be seen as pure economists, were made up of number of writers that included Antonio Serra, an Italian; Jean Bodin, a French Lawyer, Thomas Mun, a British, and Sir Josiah Child. Others were Sir John Law, Philipp Wilhelm von Hornick and Johannes Heinrich Gottlob von Justi. They had certain things in common, but differ in certain respects as they lived in different times and settings.[3]

Mercantilism, also known as colbertism in France and

---

[2] Refer to the article entitled "Mercantilism" retrieve on February 17, 2017 from https://en.m.wikipedia.org/wiki/Mercantilism
[3] Substantial part of what is presented in this chapter is adopted from my book *The Making of Economics: an Introduction to History of Economic Thought*, 2nd Edition (2012) Kano: Samarib Publishers.

cameralism in Germany, arose from the emergence of commercial capitalism in the western European countries. It was given impetus by Renaissance and the rise of Protestantism which made Europeans to begin to question the rationale of certain ideas and injunctions and to be more inclined towards materialism.

The mercantilist economic thought was centred on the empowerment of a nation state through commerce and trade, using restrictions and policies which may be detrimental to other nation states. H. L. Bhatia observed that the mercantilists were not pure economists and most of them:

> Were men of practical affairs looking at the problem not from global point of view but from the angle of an individual nation which wanted to acquire gold and silver for building up its national strength and for financing the waging of wars overseas.[4]

The means for achieving the mercantilist objectives were:

---

[4] H.L. Bhatia (1978, p18) *History of Economic Thought* (New Delhi: Vikas Publishing House PVT LTD).

a) Obtaining a balance of trade: This is achieved by exporting more goods to and importing less from other countries so that a nation gets trade surplus in terms of gold and other precious metals.

b) Increasing the supply of money in an economy: This would lead to rise in prices, a fall in interest rate and expansion of economic activities. The British mercantilists argued that the economy of England was handicapped compared to that of Holland because of high interest rate in the former country. Sir Josiah Child was quoted as saying "low interest is the natural mother of frugality, industry and arts."[5]

c) Enforcement of other regulations: these include the regulation of foreign trade, the use of national ships for cargo carrying in order to get income from insurance and freight charges, and the payment of low wages to workers in order to deter them from laziness and to cut production costs. To the mercantilists, an ill-fed labour force was compatible with a rich and strong nation, because cheap exports could be produced easily.

The physiocratic economic thought, which was scattered over a large number of writings by François Quesnay (1694 – 1774) and his associates, served as the foundation of the free economy. The thought was based on the concept of natural order coupled with economic

---

[5] *Ibid*, p 20.

individualism. The natural order of the society is regulated by the principle of individualism. The individual is seen as the best judge of his interest. According to Quesnay, the secret of the well ordered society was that a person works for others, believing that he is working for himself. Natural order brings perfect harmony of individual interest as well as that of the king and his subjects. The Physiocrats had deep respect for the ownership private property saying that man has a natural right to all goods that are suitable to his use, but the right is confined to what he could obtain through hard work. In addition, man's property is the measure of his freedom and the foremost function of laws and regulations (i.e. the *positive order*), is the protection of property rights.

The Physiocrats criticized the mercantilist thought which, for instance, favoured government regulation of economic activities (e.g. increasing export and decreasing import so as to get a favourable balance of trade). They also argued that the hope of national gain at the cost of other countries is an illusion because the cost of war that often results from economic policies that are harmful to other nations can offset the gains. They further argued that in order to be able to sell, one has to buy, and that wealth can come through production, not privation. The Physiocrats were able to realize the role of economic individualism (the invisible hand) and private ownership of the means of production as means of boosting productivity in an economy.

Adam Smith, the leading classical economist, built his economic doctrines on some of the ideas of the Physiocrats. Like the physiocrats, he supported a *laissez fair* economy and professed a philosophy of naturalism. He believed that interests of different economic units do not conflict with one another. The working of an invisible hand removes conflicting interest as each individual is made to promote an end, which though not being part of his intention, promotes the interest of the society. State regulations and monopolies are, therefore, seen as artificial barriers. Adam Smith had a better understanding of economic activities and believed that free trade would help an economy to grow. Other classical economists include David Ricardo (1772 – 1823) who formulated the theory of comparative advantage arguing that there would be gains from trade if each nation specializes in the production of the commodity in which it has a comparative cost advantage and then buys the other commodity from other nations.[6]

In 1800, a German philosopher, Karl Marx (1818 – 1883) seriously criticized the works of Adam Smith. According to Marx, free enterprise would lead to the subjugation of the working classes who would be made to revolt and take over the means of production. The free enterprise or the capitalist economic system would

---

[6] Graham Bannock; R.E Baxter and Evan Davis (1998). *The Penguin Dictionary of Economics* (6th edition). (London: Penguin Books Ltd.)

then be replaced with the socialist economic system. During 1840s and 1850s, Marx impatiently waited for a revolution against capitalism to take place. In 1848 there were revolutions but they were not successful and new ones failed to occur, this led Marx to turn to Economics to buttress his philosophy of history and demonstrate that the collapse of capitalism is inevitable. Arguing that wages given to workers do not pay them the full value of what they produce but only the lesser value for their continued subsistence, Marx uses the term *surplus value* to denote the difference between the wage and the value of a product. Marx had played down the role of capital in the creation of wealth by regarding the surplus value as the source of profit, interest and rents. He failed to realize that huge profit needs not to be based on exploitation of labour alone; it can also come from exploitation of consumers or from legitimate ways such as large scale production facilitated by technological advancement, research and development, entrepreneur's ability to withstand competition, and from expansions in sales which the use of the Internet other communication systems makes possible today.

Abu Zaid Waliyyul al-Din Abdurrahman Ibn Khaldun (1332-1406) supported *laissez fair* several years before Adam Smith. He did not want government to participate in commerce but wanted it to regulate market through the institution of *hisba*, which is used to check fraud and deceptions in the measurement and weighing of goods. The work of *hisba* is similar to the present day agencies of government that protect consumers from harmful or low quality food, drugs and other commodities. Ibn Khaldun observes that the greater the population of a society, the greater the market for goods and services, the greater the production level. When people become very rich their love for leisure increases and productivity would begin to decline. On fiscal policy, Ibn Khaldun argues that government spending has to be kept high because businesses would slump when government reduces spending. Before W.W. Rostow and Karl Marx made their theories on the stages of economic development, Ibn Khaldun had identified and explained the following stages of economic development:[7]

i. Primitive stage: At this stage, nomads whose main occupation is rearing animals and villagers who till the soil for food exist. The needs of these people are limited to food, shelter and clothes. There is a collective ownership of resources and a strong group feeling (*asabiyah*). Moreover, the people are more religious and courageous than urban dwellers. The stage is also characterized by minimal crime and simple division of labour.

ii. Town Stage: This stage is characterized by an improvement in the talents and skills of people which enable them to utilize

---

[7] Sule A Gusau (1991) "Thoughts and Views of Ibn Khaldun on Economics" in *Economic Thoughts of Seven Great Muslim Scholars* edited by Sule Ahmed Gusau. Printed by the Usmanu Danfodiyo University, Sokoto.

resources provided by God. More refined crafts exist. Private ownership is institutionalized, group feeling declines, crime rate rises and inequality emerges.

iii. Stage of Urbanism: This is a stage of cities and urban centres. There are significant refinements of occupations and an improvement in the standard of living. Trade and industry become the major means of acquiring wealth. There is a deep – seated inequality of income which promotes greed, jealousy and crime. Indulgence in luxuries damages the souls of people and they engage in fraud, theft, perjury and dealing in usury. Cities attract dubious characters while group feeling almost disappears.

iv. Stage of Decline: At this stage, luxury increases the population of the cities and this leads to additional wealth. Later on, excessive affluence generates disincentive to work among people. Group feeling is totally eroded while injustice and crime reach an unprecedented level. Confiscation of peoples' properties, high tax and the disincentive to work would lead to a decline in productivity and subsequently to famine.

In France, Leon Walras (1834 – 1910) worked out a mathematical expression to show how each part of an economy was related to others. Pareto (1848 – 1923), who regarded mathematics as an efficient way of investigation of economic phenomenon, believed that economic forces work towards the attainment of an equilibrium.

The great depression of the 1930s led a British economist, John Maynard Keynes (1883-1946) to attack the idea that free markets would always lead to prosperity and full employment. He argues that government spending could bring an end to depression. During the mid – 1900s the monetarist emerged. Their spokesman was Milton Friedman. According to them monetary policy should be used to stabilize prices and promote economic growth.[8]

Presently, economists base their theories and arguments on case studies and empirical research. They emphasize the use of mathematics and statistics in analyzing economic phenomenon. However, recent scholars such as Rongxing Guo, a Chinese economist, rightly emphasize the importance of considering culture, which embodies ethnicity, language, religion, etc, in economic analysis. As he points out, mainstream economists have failed to accept the significant existence of cultural influences on economic performance despite the fact that economic activities could not be conducted independently of a given cultural context. The

---

[8] *World Bank Encyclopedia* Vol. 6, 1980.

economy, he declares, "is as much a cultural site as any other part of society – family, community or school."[9] There is sense in his thesis because culture plays a major role in promoting or inhibiting economic activities and development. Culture influences peoples' behavior and attitude to work, production, consumption, trade and exchange, to mention a few.

From the brief account of the evolution of economics given above, it could be seen that economists were and are still divided into camps. Put in another way, they belong to different schools of thought. Secondly, economics is a dynamic science that is changing continuously to address prevailing problems and suit the circumstances of the day.

---

[9] Rongxing Guo (2006, p 78) *Cultural Influences on Economic Analysis: Theory and Empirical Evidence* (New York: Palgrave Macmillan).

CHAPTER TWO

PROTECTIONISM AS AN ELEMENT OF MERCANTILISM

This chapter provides a general explanation of mercantilism, an economic system practiced in Europe from 16th to 18th century, which is almost synonymous with protectionism because of its self-centered and antagonistic features. The chapter will examine the features of mercantilism, its benefits as well as criticisms against it. The goal of the chapter is to show how protectionism is visibly manifested by the features mercantilism and the main ways of achieving its goals.

Mercantilism became popular in Europe during the 1500s. It replaced the older, feudal economic system in Western Europe, especially in Netherlands, France and England. In Britain, the Sugar Act of 1764 introduced high customs for sugar and molasses imported from outside. The country's Navigations Act of 1651 was also implemented to ensure that foreign vessels would not be able to do trade along its coast.[10] Many nations in Europe applied the theory of mercantilism throughout the late Renaissance and early modern period. In France, King Louis XIV followed the

---

[10] *Mercantilism*. Retrieved on February 12, 2017 from http://www.investopedia.com/terms/m/mercantilism.asp

guidance of Jean Baptiste Colbert, his controller general of finances from 1665–1683. In England, the first large-scale and integrative approach to mercantilism was started during the Elizabethan Era (1558–1603). The most notable people in establishing the English mercantilist system include Gerard de Malynes and Thomas Mun, who first articulated the Elizabethan system which was developed further by Josiah Child. Mercantilism was the economic version of warfare that used economics as a means for warfare. It was a form of economic nationalism.[11]

While the term "mercantile system" was used by its foremost critic, Adam Smith, the term "mercantilism" had been used earlier by Mirabeau. Adam Smith coined the term "mercantile system" which literally means "trade system" to describe the system of political economy meant to enrich a nation by restraining imports and encouraging exports. The mercantilist system was created on the belief that a nation's wealth and power were best realized through increasing exports and accumulating precious metals such as gold and silver. Gold, silver and other precious metals were regarded indispensable to a nation's wealth. A nation that lacks them has to obtain them through trade. Impressed by the fact that precious metals, especially

---

[11] *Mercantilism.* Retrieved on February 12, 2017 from https://en.m.wikipedia.org/wiki/Mercantilism

gold, were in universal demand, early mercantilist writers believed that quantities of gold and silver were the measure of a nation's wealth. This belief is called bullionism. They also identified money with wealth, so under a mercantilist system a nation ought to sell more than it buys in order to accumulate bullion.[12]

In the mercantilist system, favourable trade balances, that is, an excess of exports over imports, were believed to be a must. Mercantilism encouraged governmental regulation of a nation's economy for the purpose of augmenting state power at the expense of rival nations. Mercantilism was the economic equivalent of political absolutism.[13] Many British writers, including Mun and Misselden, were merchants while many of the writers from other countries were public officials.

High tariffs, especially on manufactured goods, are an almost universal feature of mercantilist policy. Laura LaHaye, an adjunct professor at the Illinois Institute of Technology and former research economist with the

---

[12] *Mercantilism*. Retrieved on February 12, 2017 from
http://www.newworldencyclopedia.org/entry/Mercantilism

[13] *Mercantilism*. Retrieved on February 12, 2017 from
https://www.britannica.com/topic/mercantilism

General Agreement on Tariffs and Trade, writes that "The mercantile system served the interests of merchants and producers such as the British East India Company, whose activities were protected or encouraged by the state."[14] By the beginning of the 16th century, European financial theorists had begun to understand the importance of the merchant class in generating wealth. The state should franchise out the leading merchants to create exclusive monopolies and cartels to be controlled by the government and to serve as an arm of its interests. In return, the government would use regulations, subsidies and, if needed, military to protect corporations of the merchants from domestic and foreign competition.[15]

The goals of mercantilism were mainly achieved through the following: [16]

a) Imposing high tariffs on the importation of finished goods that competed with local

---

[14] Laura LaHay (2008) *Mercantilism*. Liberty Fund, Inc. Retrieved on February 16, 2017 from http://www.econlib.org/library/Enc/Mercantilism.html

[15] *Mercantilism*. Retrieved on February 12, 2017 from http://www.investopedia.com/terms/m/mercantilism.asp

[16] *Mercantilism*. Retrieved on February 12, 2017 from https://en.m.wikipedia.org/wiki/Mercantilism and Laura LaHay (2008) *Mercantilism*. Liberty Fund, Inc Retrieved on February 16, 2017 from http://www.econlib.org/library/Enc/Mercantilism.html

manufacturers; and imposing low or no taxes on the importation of raw materials or exotic products.

b) Imposing low or no taxes on the export of finished goods; and imposing high taxes on the exportation of raw materials.

c) Seeking new markets for domestic manufactured products so as to artificially increase the demand for domestic production.

d) Prohibiting export of tools and capital equipment and the emigration of skilled labour that would allow foreign countries and the colonies of the home country to compete in the production of manufactured goods.

Benefits of Mercantilism

Mercantilist policies had a positive impact on Britain helping it to turn into the world's dominant trader and global power. The Italian city-state of Venice, which monopolized the Mediterranean pilgrim and spice trades, prohibited the importation of finished products and forced all Venetian naval traffic to make a stop in Venice regardless of the cargoes final destination. This ensured additional economic activities within Venice and enriched it at its consumers' expense.

The Great Depression of the 1930s created doubts about the effectiveness and stability of free market economies. At the same time, an emerging body of economic thought ranging from Keynesianism to Marxist centrally planned economy gave governments a role in the control of economic affairs. Furthermore, Keynes and other economists of that time realized the importance of balance of payments in international trade and regarded favourable balance of trade as desirable. Since the 1930s, nations closely monitored the inflow and outflow of capital. Adam Smith praised the Navigation Acts of 1651, which prohibited foreign vessels from engaging in coastal trade in England, because they expanded the British merchant fleet and played a central role in turning Britain into the world's naval and economic superpower from the 18th century onward. Some economists argued that protecting infant industries, while causing short-term harm, can be beneficial to an economy in the long run.

Criticisms against Mercantilism

The first school of economic thought to completely reject mercantilism was that of the physiocrats. As advocates of laissez-faire, the physiocrats saw no distinction between domestic and foreign trade and believed that all trade was beneficial both to the trader and the public. As stated earlier, many British writers about mercantilism, including Mun and Misselden, were merchants, so it is not surprising that Adams Smith, who is considered to be greatest critic of mercantilism, to perceive the mercantile system as a gigantic conspiracy by manufacturers and merchants against consumers. The system served the interests of merchants and producers such as the British East India Company whose activities were protected or encouraged by the state. Again, in his famous book, *The Wealth of Nations*, Smith demonstrated that trade, when freely initiated, benefited both parties and that specialization in production allowed for economies of scale which improved efficiency and growth. He also pointed out that the collusive relationship between government and industry was harmful to the general population. [17]

Other critics such as Dudley North, John Locke and David Hume damaged much of mercantilism making it unpopular during the eighteenth century. The mercantilists failed to understand the notions of absolute advantage and comparative advantage, which were expounded in 1817 by David Ricardo. David Hume noted the impossibility of achieving the mercantilists' goal of a constant positive balance of

---

[17] *Ibid.*

trade because as bullion enters into a country, its supply would increase while its value would decline steadily in relation to other goods. Conversely, in the country exporting the bullion, its value would slowly rise. In the end, it would no longer be cost-effective to export goods from the high-price country to the low-price country. When this happens, the balance of trade would reverse itself. The mercantilists fundamentally misunderstood this.[18]

The mercantilist idea that all trade was a zero sum game, in which each side was trying to beat the other in a ruthless competition, was said to be integrated into the works of Thomas Hobbes. This idea is a fallacy. Trade between two nations, for instance, Nigeria buying machinery and tools for textile production from China, can result in a win-win transaction that brings benefits to both nations.

During the mercantilist period, military conflicts between nation-states were more frequent and more extensive than at any other time in history. Since it is impossible for every country to have a surplus of exports, the basis of mercantilism was doomed for

---

[18] This comes from the work of Ekelund Robert B., and Robert D. Tollison cited in the article *Mercantilism*, retrieved from on February 18, 2017 from http://www.newworldencyclopedia.org/entry/Mercantilism

eventual failure. Belief in mercantilism began to fade in the late eighteenth century as the arguments of Adam Smith and the other classical economists won favour in the British Empire. The signing of the General Agreement on Tariffs and Trade (GATT) in 1947 marked the official recognition of the need to establish an international order of multilateral free trade while the establishment of the World Trade Organization (WTO) is meant to enforce the agreed-on rules of international trade.

Laura LaHaye observes that the argument that a current account deficit is bad for a country is among the false tenets of mercantilism that remain today. This deficit can come through borrowing from or selling assets to the rest of the world to finance expenditure on imports in excess of export revenue. Even when this results in an increase of net foreign indebtedness, it will promote economic wealth if the spending is for productive purposes giving greater return than what is forgone on the assets exchanged. Another fallacy is the thought that imports decrease domestic employment which labor unions have used to justify protection from imports coming from in low-wage countries.[19]

---

[19] Laura LaHay (2008) *Mercantilism*. Liberty Fund, Inc Retrieved on February 16, 2017 from http://www.econlib.org/library/Enc/Mercantilism.html

Conclusion

From the description of the features of mercantilism and the main ways of achieving its goals, it could be observed that protectionism has been an important element of mercantilism. Protectionism was manifested in the forms of regulation of a nation's economy for the purpose of augmenting state power at the expense of rival nations, imposing high tariffs on the importation of finished goods to protect the interest of local manufacturers, restraining imports and encouraging exports. Other forms of protectionism were banning the export of tools and capital equipment and the emigration of skilled labour to other nations with view to discouraging them from competing with firms producing goods and services in the country implementing mercantilist policies. From the arguments in support of mercantilism and the criticism against it, protectionism, especially in the period of globalization when the world is reduced to a global village, is largely harmful to the global economy. It can spur misunderstanding and fan the embers of hatred among members of the international community.

CHAPTER THREE

ANATOMY OF THE GLOBAL ECONOMY IN THE ERA OF ADVANCED GLOBALIZATION

Introduction

This chapter describes the anatomy or framework of the global economy in the context of advanced globalization by citing relevant literature and providing an over simplified example of a global economy made up of five nations. The chapter also restates the need for the adoption of globoeconomics as a third level economic analysis to reflect the realities brought about by globalization, a phenomenon that has been in existence for a long time and which nations cannot dismiss, but should rather learn to live with.[20]

Definitions and Features of Globalization

The Cambridge Dictionary defines term globalization in its two senses. In the first sense, globalization refers to "the increase of trade around the world, especially by large companies producing and trading goods in many

---

[20] This chapter draws its main substances from the author's earlier work entitled *Globoeconomics: A solution to nation's economic problems,* but with certain modifications to update its thesis.

different countries," in the second, it means "a situation in which available goods and services, or social and cultural influences, gradually become similar in all parts of the world." The first definition is what matters here because it is connected with protectionism and the global economy. [21]

The Merriam-Webster Dictionary defines globalization as "the development of an increasingly integrated global economy marked especially by free trade, free flow of capital, and the tapping of cheaper foreign labor markets." This beautiful definition is very relevant to the subject matter and concerns of this book. In addition, it is comprehensive in terms of including some salient features of globalization, namely free trade, free flow of capital from one nation to another and tapping cheaper foreign labour markets.[22]

The Business Dictionary explains globalization as "the opening of local and nationalistic perspectives to a broader outlook of an interconnected and interdependent world with free transfer of capital,

---

[21] http://dictionary.cambridge.org/dictionary/english/globalization Accessed on February 22, 2017.

[22] https://www.merriam-webster.com/dictionary/globalization Accessed on February 22, 2017.

goods, and services across national frontiers." This definition also captures some salient features of globalization with an addition "of an interconnected and interdependent world."[23]

One interesting thing to note about the first two definitions is that globalization is portrayed as an ongoing phenomenon. Describing it as "the increase of trade" and as "the development of an increasingly integrated global economy", imply that it has been in existence, but has now reached a higher stage of development.

The irony about globalization, says Jagdish Khatri, Chairholder-UNESCO Network Chair, is that it has been blamed for the problems which it actually tries to eradicate. Globalization, he writes, has been one of the most debated, most resisted and most blamed phenomenon all over the world, giving birth to many movements opposing its provisions and implementation. It is seen as the cause of almost all social and economic ills prevailing in different societies, even though the ills were there centuries ago. Khatri beautifully identified ten features of

---

[23] http://www.businessdictionary.com/definition/globalization.html
Accessed on February 22, 2017.

globalization. First, it is not a new, Western concept because even the Indian scriptures have mentioned *"Vasudhaiva Kutumbakam"* and viewed the world as a small global village of linked families. Second, it is basically a mindset that is ready to put the whole universe into its scheme of things, open to receive all ideas and take the whole globe as an area of operation. Third, globalization is an opportunity opening all other markets in the whole world for goods and services. Fourth, it means interdependence as it creates a culture of interdependence among nations because no country can be totally independent, not requiring anything from any other country. Globalization also means caring and sharing because the world today is more united and concerned about common problems such as global warming, terrorism, malnutrition, natural disasters, etc, than it was in the past; it puts technology in service of mankind as communication technology has turned the world into a global village, bringing people nearer. Globalization is inevitable and irreversible, in fact, attempts by fundamentalist forces all over the world to oppose and stop it over past quarter century have failed because as is rightly said, "You cannot stop the advent of an idea whose time has come". Another feature of globalization is that it has linked politics with Economics. In earlier times, political ideologies and the strength of relations have determined the fate of people, and economics was made subservient to politics, in the new era, it is economics (employment generation and public welfare, etc.) that determines the need and strength of relations between nations. Globalization also means raised standards of living as consumers are having more choices from quality items and with no boundary restrictions on flow of goods and services, and the markets have turned from 'Sellers Market' to 'Buyers Market'. This raises the standard of living for vast populations across the world. Finally, globalization demands and respects excellence because the opportunities which globalization gives to all nations, open the field for excellent companies, products and people from anywhere to showcase their excellence and win over markets and contracts.[24]

The Anatomy the Global Economy

D. Keet explains that the contemporary world conceives the global economy in four different ways. First, the global economy is seen as an international economic

---

[24] For details refer to Prof. Jagdish Khatri's paper Ten Basic Characteristics of Globalization, published on January 6, 2015 and retrieved on February 22, 2017 from https://www.linkedin.com/pulse/ten-basic-characteristics-globalization-prof-jagdish-khatri

system within which economies of individual nations *have been or are very rapidly being absorbed and disappearing.* This is because the economic system is characterized by porous borders and limited policy options that are *losing viability and relevance.* Secondly, it is seen as the sum of *complex interactions* between national economies. Thirdly, the contemporary world conceives the global economy as a *complex combination* of national economies or national economies within regional economies, upon which transnational economic agents and international institutions and regulations operate. Lastly, it is viewed as a dynamic combination of a distinctive supra-national global economy manifested by the independent operations of transnational economic agencies and actors which act upon and interact with the economies of individual nations and with regional economies *while being uncommitted or unattached to any specific national economy* (all italics indicate the actual words used by Keet).[25]

From the above, it is clear that economies of individual nations are now being absorbed into the global economy or simply disappearing. Put in another way,

---

[25] Keet, D. 1999, *Globalization and Regionalization: Contradictory Tendencies, Counteractive Tactics or Strategic Possibilities.* (Braamfontein: The Foundation for Global Dialogue)

national economies are losing their distinctive qualities. It is further indicated that national economies are losing viability and relevance. The global economy, as depicted above, is characterized by complex interactions between national economies and the global economy, and by complex combinations of national economies with regional economies, transnational economic actors and international institutions. The economy of Germany, for instance, interacts and is acted upon by the European economy, which is a regional economy and by the global economy and the international economic institutions such as the World Bank and the International Monetary Fund (I.M.F.). Macroeconomic policy in Germany could be less effective and meaningful without the consideration of the influences of the European economy and the global economy. The independent operations of transnational economic agencies and actors, being uncommitted and unattached to national economics also have to be taken into consideration.

K. Griffin and A.R. Khan have adduced a number of points to show the impact of globalization on macroeconomic policy and analysis. First, with the integration of states into something that is close to a single economic system, the ability of a nation to impose its will on other economic factors, notably transnational firms, is weakened. Second, it has become more difficult for a country to impose its authority on persons and entities that fall theoretically, under its jurisdiction. This is due to increased mobility of goods, assets and even people across national boundaries. Thirdly, internalization of currency markets has made the control of money supply by central banks of nations more difficult. Fourth, nations find it difficult to determine nominal rates of interest and the term structure of interest rates due to the integration of bond markets. Fifth, transfer pricing used by large organizations for transaction between semi-autonomous divisions supplying components to one another, allows transnational corporations to shift profit tax liabilities from countries with high taxation to countries with law taxation. This affects the fiscal policy of nations. Sixth, the ability of large corporations to locate and relocate fixed investment almost anywhere in the world limits the power of a nation to regulate industry through taxation, minimum wage regulation, environmental control, etc. Seventh, international markets have eroded political sovereignty of nations, as they are unable to act unilaterally in pursuance of economic goals.[26]

The above seven points indicate the diverse impacts of

---

[26] Griffin, K and Khan, A.R. (1992) *Globalization and the Developing World: An Essay on the International Dimensions of Development in the Post-Cold War Era.* (Geneva: United Nations Research Institute for Social Development.)

globalization on macroeconomic policy and analysis made to achieve certain macroeconomic goals or address macroeconomic problems. Even the developed nations are not free from the effects of globalization on their economies as Griffin and Khan observe:[27]

> No one would pretend, for example, that the United States in 1992 is just as capable of regulating its internal economic affairs as it was in 1952. It clearly is not: globalization has made a difference.

To further support the thesis that globalization is undermining the relevance and effectiveness of macroeconomic policy and analysis, the views of specialists in international economics could be of value. In this regard, P.R. Krugman and M. Obstafeld have observed that the inherent inter dependence of open national economies sometimes bring difficulties for governments seeking to achieve macroeconomic policy goals such as full employment and price level stability. Secondly, after describing the international economy as comprising sovereign nations with freedom to choose their own economic policies, they went ahead to say:

> Unfortunately, in an integrated world economy one country's economic policies

---

[27] Ibid, p 64.

usually affect other countries as well. For example, when Germany's Bundesbank raised interest rates in 1990 – a step it took to control the possible inflationary impact of the reunification of West and East Germany – it helped precipitate a recession in the rest of Eastern Europe.[28]

By talking about open national economies and an integrated world economy, Krugman and Obstfeld are simply referring to the global economy, which operates within the context of globalization. Their views also lend support to the thesis that globalization limits the relevance and effectiveness of macroeconomic policy and analysis.

The existence of digital currency or digital money also forms part of the framework of the global economy because they make borderless transfer-of-ownership possible even though central banks of many nations do not accept this development. The digital currency is an Internet-based form of currency or medium of exchange which is distinct from physical money. It makes instantaneous transactions and borderless transfer-of-ownership possible. Its origin dates back to the 1990s

---

[28] Krugman, P. R. and Obstfeld, M.(undated). *International Economics: Theory and Policy.* (Addison Wesley Longman Inc.) p.7.

Dot-com bubble. The E-gold founded in 1996 and backed by gold is among the first digital currencies. Recent interest in cryptocurrencies, that is, digital tokens that rely on cryptography for chaining together digital signatures of token transfers, peer-to-peer networking and decentralization, has given impetus to new interest in digital currencies, with *bitcoin*, introduced in 2009, being the most popular among them.[29]

The Need for Globoeconomics: the Third Level of Economic Analysis

Sequel to the growing irrelevance and ineffectiveness of macroeconomic policy and analysis, another level of economic analysis that will suit the circumstances brought by the advancement that globalization has reached in recent times, becomes necessary. This means macroeconomic analysis could be ineffective if made with reference to a single country without considering other economic actors and forces in the global economy.

Joseph E. Stiglitz, a Professor at Columbia University and the recipient of the Nobel Prize in Economics in

---

[29] Ladislav Mecir (editor) (2017) "Digital currency" *Wikipedia.* Retrieved on February 22, 2017 from https://en.m.wikipedia.org/wiki/Digital_currency

2001, had made this suggestion in relation to the 2009 global financial crisis:

> A global downturn requires a global response. But so far our responses – to stimulate and regulate the global economy – have largely been framed at the national level and often take insufficient account of the effect on others. The result is that there is less coordination than there should be, as well as a smaller and less well-designed stimulus than is optimal.[30]

Griffin and Khan had used the term "global macro economy" probably as something to receive the attention of economists instead of the Keynesian macroeconomics, but they failed to provide its definition and goals. Krugman and Obstfeld, two scholars of International Economics, have also talked about the importance of what they termed "international macroeconomic policy coordination." Perhaps these terms could be construed as their own yearnings for something that can at least supplement if not replace macroeconomic analysis due to the influences of globalization.

---

[30] Stiglitz, Joseph E. (2009) "A Global Recovery for a Global Recession" *The Nation* retrieved on October 8, 2010 from http://www.thenation.com/article/global-recovery-global-recession

It is better for economists to come up with a new a concept for a macroeconomic analysis that reflects globalization instead of "global macro-economy", or the "international macroeconomic policy coordination." This is because policy coordination deals with coordinating macroeconomic policies already formulated by individual nations without necessarily taking the forces of globalization into consideration. Coordination should, indeed, start at the level of policy conception and formulation, and continue up to the levels of policy implementation, appraisal and review. When the Leaders of the Group of Twenty (G-20) held an initial meeting in Washington on November 15, 2008 on the economic recession prevailing at that time, they declared that the major underlying factors that lead to the current situation were, among others, inconsistent and insufficiently coordinated macroeconomic policies, and inadequate structural reforms.[31]

The term globoeconomics could conveniently be used to refer to the third level of economic analysis, the first and second being microeconomics and macroeconomics, respectively. Globoeconomics has already been defined as

> the study of macro-economic variables and

---

[31] Online Wall Street Journal.com *G-20 Statement Following Crisis Talks* http://online.wsj.com/article/SB122677642316131071.html accessed on 26 December 2008.

policies of a nation, region or the entire globe as they influence or are influenced by macroeconomic variables and policies of other nations or regions as a result of globalization.[32]

Globoeconomics involves the study of macroeconomic variables of a nation as they relate and interact with similar variables in other nations. It also studies macroeconomic variables in regional economies such as the European or Asian economies as they relate to and interact with similar variables in individual nations, other regional and sub regional economies and in the entire global economy. Thirdly, as the world is increasingly emerging as a global village, globoeconomics studies macroeconomic variables in the entire global economy, for instance, attempts can be made to determine the global inflation rate, global level of output, unemployment, etc, with a view to achieving desired economic goals such as eradication of global poverty, promoting global welfare and increasing global consumption and sales of certain goods and services.

Globoeconomic policies are macroeconomic policies that take in to account the forces and requirements of

---

[32] Sulaiman, Sa'idu (2004) *The Impact of Globalization on Macroeconomic Policies of Nations and the Need for the Adoption of Globoeconomics,* unpublished paper.

globalization from the time they are conceived and formulated to the time they are implemented, coordinated, appraised and reviewed. Globoeconomic policies have the potential of moving economic activities and goals in the entire world towards a unity of purpose and benefits. This is because it is characterized by interdependence, which is analogous to the interdependence existing among parts of the human body. A faulty fiscal policy in South Africa or Egypt, for instance, can exacerbate depression, and this can lower demand for both domestic and foreign goods thereby affecting sales, productivity and employment in the domestic economy and in the economies of nations trading with that country.

Globoeconomics analysis should aim at achieving the following major goals: [33]

(a) Providing a fair and comprehensive description of economic phenomenon in individual nations, regions and at the global level by taking into account the prevailing forces of globalization. Economic phenomenon such as exchange rate, level of capacity utilization, level of sales, growth rate, etc, should be described in the context of globalization.

---

[33] *Ibid.*

(b) Formulating policies, designing models and strategies for moving the economies of nations, regions and the entire globe forward; and minimizing their economic problems on the bases of achievements made in relation to the first goal.

(c) Globoeconomics, because of its tendency to move economic activities towards a unity of purpose, should promote interdependence, peaceful co-existence and mutual benefits among nations.

These goals cannot be achieved if there is protectionism or there is no fair play in the global economic game and competition, and also if weak nations are not assisted to utilize resources at their disposals and in line with their socio-cultural peculiarities and economic needs.

An Illustration of the Anatomy of the Global Economy

For simplicity it is assumed that there five nations in the world and each has one major economic activity as the chief source of its income. Thus, agriculture, mining of petroleum, production of automobiles, manufacture of consumables, and tourism are considered to be the mainstays of the economies of United States of

America (USA), Nigeria, Japan, United Kingdom and Thailand, respectively. Each country pursues its economic activity on the basis of its natural endowments, technological development and the comparative advantage it has in relation to its economic activity.

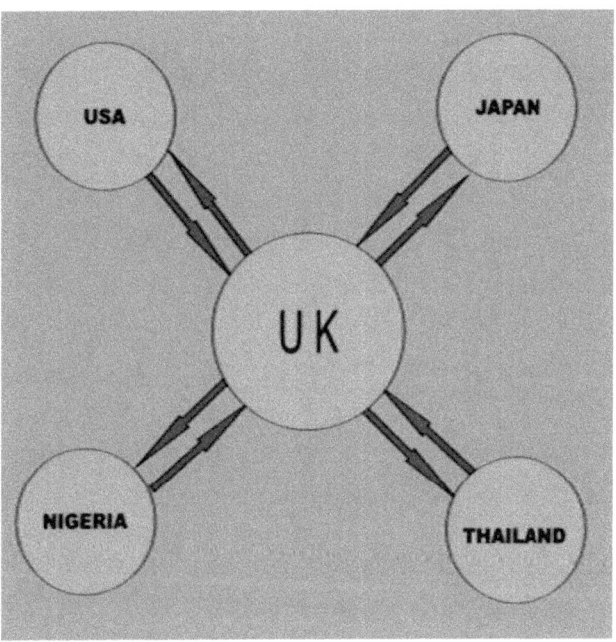

Fig.1. Economic interdependence among the members of a five-nation world

United Kingdom is put in the middle of the other countries to show how its economy relates with the economies of the other countries. The arrows originating from United Kingdom indicate what goes out from it to other nations, while those originating from USA, Nigeria, Japan, and Thailand indicate what it gets from these countries. Each country can, therefore, assume the position of the United Kingdom in the diagram to indicate how its economy helps and depends on the economies of other nations.

In the example given, United Kingdom manufactures consumables such as chemicals, lubricants, processed foods, stationery and drugs. It imports petroleum from Nigeria and farm produce from USA. It also imports vehicles from Japan for distributing its finished goods. With an increase in economic activities and prosperity in this country, its demand for these imports will be on the increase and the number of tourists wishing to visit Thailand from the United Kingdom will also increase. So when the economy of the United Kingdom prospers, it will boost economic activities in the other countries.

Low domestic and foreign demand for manufactures from the United Kingdom will lead to low demand for farm produce from USA, automobiles from Japan and petroleum from Nigeria. Moreover, a downturn in the economic activities in the United Kingdom will reduce the number of tourists willing and capable of visiting Thailand. Low demand for petroleum from Nigeria can be aggravated by low demand for automobiles and by the use of alternative fuel for running them, this will result in less income among Nigerians and subsequently a fall in their demand for other goods and services produced by the other four nations.

From this simple illustration, it could be seen that with the ever increasing forces of globalization, macroeconomic policy in a single nation with a view to increasing output and employment or reduce inflation rate is becoming increasingly ineffective. So nations have to sit together to fashion out a mutually beneficial goboeconomic policy. With the simplified example of a five-nation world, the affected nations can, for instance, meet to agree on the following policies:

a) *Stimulating domestic demand for goods and services in each country*: this can be through the means of government spending in form increase in public works (roads, dams, schools, electricity, etc) upward review of workers' salaries and allowances for students, etc. A deficit budget is needed in a period of recession so that the increase in government expenditure can come through borrowing from local and foreign sources depending on what will be done with the money. Projects that require foreign exchange can require external loans while projects that can be executed with local resources do not require external loans. The disadvantage of borrowing by government is that the prevailing interest rate may go up, thus increasing the cost of capital for investors. Increase in money supply by printing additional money and using it to increase government spending is another alternative for a deficit budget. Its disadvantage is that it will lead to inflation if the amount of money supplied exceeds the level of output in an economy. In some developing and underdeveloped nations, reliable measurement of their levels of output does not exist as most informal economic activities are left out in determining their GDPs.[34] It could be argued that the use of money in providing basic infrastructure could lead to rise in GDP as well as lower the cost of production facing industries thus reducing the level of inflation. Some leaders and economists tend to emphasize a control of inflation rate even if such control will bring hardship to people. Achieving a low inflation rate is simply a means to an end, not an end in itself. The end is to increase the standard of living of people though good nutrition and health care,

---

[34] Gross Domestic Product (GDP) is the total value of goods and services produced in a country over a period of time, it may be calculated by adding up the value of all goods and services produced; the expenditure on goods and services at the time of sale; or producers' incomes from the sale of goods or services (Gross Domestic Product. *Microsoft® Encarta® 2006* [DVD]. Redmond, WA: Microsoft Corporation, 2005.)

education, etc. That is why development is now measured in terms of the Human Development Index[35], not low inflation rate or the GDP only.

b) *Curtailing protectionism*: there are two types of protectionism. Use of tariffs and taxes to discourage imports from other countries as well as outright banning of importation of certain goods can be referred to as primary protectionism. Secondary protectionism is any attempt to achieve complete self-reliance in providing home made goods coupled with conduct of research on the production of alternatives to goods being imported from other nations even if the nation doing so lacks a comparative advantage in producing them. Therefore nations wishing to formulate an effective globoeconomic policy have to agree on the level of protectionisms they can tolerate in view of their peculiarities and needs as individual nations, and on the basis of their collective goal of attacking global recession.

---

[35] Human Development Index (HDI) is an estimate of living standards published for the first time in 1990 by the United Nations Development Program. It uses a scale of 1 to 100 and takes into account GDP per head, adult literacy, and life expectancy.

This is what makes trade agreements like GATT useful.

c) *Setting goals and targets as well as identifying means for achieving them:* desired levels of global output, employment, economic growth, etc, and specifying the contribution to be made by each country in relation to these goals and targets are also part of the policies to be agreed upon by the affected nations.

CHAPTER FOUR

LESSONS FROM THE AMERICAN EXPERIENCE

Introduction

President Donald John Trump, the 45th President of the United States of America, is currently seen as pursuing protectionist economic policies even though his policy of putting American interest first could earn him the title of a true nationalist on account of his temerity in expressing his love and deep concern for American people, more especially, the workers that lost their jobs to people in other countries.

In the first quarter of 2017, the best source of lessons on peoples' experience with protectionism and its likely repercussions on the global economy should come from the Trump's protectionist policies captured in his campaign speeches, administrative policies and the executive orders he had so far signed. This chapter provides a brief description of Trump's protectionist policies, their perceived repercussions on the global economy and the reactions they received from international organizations, world leaders, businesses and Americans in general. This is followed by statement of lessons from the American experience with the policies.

Trump's Protectionist Policies

Trump's Policies from his Campaign Promises

Trump's campaign speech entitled "Declaring American Economic Independence" delivered at Alumisource Factory in Monessen, Pennsylvania, on June 28, 2017, contained his campaign promises which reflected his protectionist views. The following paragraphs encapsulate the main messages in the historic speech:[36]

1) *The Effect of Globalization on American Economy:* Trump said the wave of globalization had wiped out the American middle class and left its millions of workers with nothing but poverty and heartache. He expressed his support for Britain leaving the European Union, saying, "Our friends in Britain recently voted to take back control of their economy, politics and borders. I was on the right side of that issue - with the people." Trump further observed that America became the world's

---

[36] Donald J. Trump (2016) *Declaring American Economic Independence,* retrieved on February 12, 2017 from

https://assets.donaldjtrump.com/DJT_DeclaringAmericanEconomicIndependence.pdf

dominant economy by being the world's dominant producer. It later changed its policy from promoting development in America, to promoting development in other nations by allowing "foreign countries to subsidize their goods, devalue their currencies, violate their agreements and cheat in every way imaginable." With this trillions of dollars and millions of American jobs flowed overseas. Today, America imports nearly $800 billion more in goods than it exports. This politician–made disaster comes from a leadership class that adores globalism more than Americanism.

2) *NAFTA and China's Entrance into the World Trade Organization:* Trump regards NAFTA as the worst trade deal in history, and argues that China's entrance into the World Trade Organization had made the greatest jobs theft in history possible. Bill Clinton signed NAFTA in 1993 and also lobbied for China's disastrous entry into the World Trade Organization. Trump stated that half of America's entire manufacturing trade deficit in goods with the world was the result of its trade with China.

5. *Trade Reform and the Negotiation of Great Trade Deals as the Quickest Way to Bring Jobs Back:* Trump posits that understanding why trade reform creates jobs requires understanding how all nations grow and prosper. Substantial trade deficits directly reduce America's Gross Domestic Product since 2002 – the year after it fully opened its markets to

Chinese imports. GDP growth rate has been cut almost in half. For Americans, it means that for every one percent of GDP growth America fails to generate in any given year, it also fails to create over one million jobs. Thus America's "job creation deficit" due to slower growth since 2002 is well over 20 million jobs.

4. *The Trans-Pacific Partnership as the Greatest Danger:* Trump perceives the Trans-Pacific Partnership (TPP) as a potential death blow for American manufacturing. It would give up all the country's economic leverage to an international commission that would put the interests of foreign countries above that of Americans, further open American markets to aggressive currency cheaters and make it easier for its trading competitors to ship cheap subsidized goods into U.S. markets. Trump called the attention of his audience to his prediction of China's indirect or direct entry into the TPP, he says, "Mark my words, China will enter the TPP through the back door at a later date. That's not all. Mark my words, China will be in this deal at a later date, if we don't stop it -- they will come in through the back door." To show his pessimism for having a reformed TPP, he declares that "There is no way to "fix" the TPP. We need bilateral trade deals. We do not need to enter into another massive international agreement that ties us up and binds us down."

5. *Steps which Trump Administration will follow to quickly Change the Failed Trade Policy:* Trump explains 7 steps he would pursue right away to bring back jobs to Americans. The first four steps are:

a) Withdrawing the United States from the Trans-Pacific Partnership which has not yet been ratified.
b) Appointing the toughest and smartest trade negotiators to fight on behalf of American workers.
c) Directing the Secretary of Commerce to identify every violation of trade agreements a foreign country is currently using to harm American workers, and directing all appropriate agencies to use every tool under American and international law to end these abuses.
d) Telling the NAFTA partners that Trump intends to immediately renegotiate the terms of that agreement to get a better deal for American workers. Not just a little bit better deal, but a lot better, and if the partners do not agree to a renegotiation, then a notice that America intends to withdraw from the deal, as provided under Article 2205 of the NAFTA agreement, will be submitted.

Trump's Economic Policies as Reflected in the Policy Documents of his Administration

Trump's trade deal policy is based on the premise that for long the interest of insiders and Washington elite has taken precedence over that of hard-working Americans. This has resulted in closures of factories and good–paying jobs moving overseas. Trump's policy, therefore, seeks to put American workers and businesses first when it comes to trade. With tough and fair trade agreements, international trade can be used to boost American economy and return the millions of jobs lost to other nations. The strategy for achieving this will start with a withdrawal from the Trans-Pacific Partnership and ensuring that new trade deals are in the interest of American workers. The second is renegotiating NAFTA, and if other partners do not accept this, withdrawing from NAFTA. In addition, the United States will crack down on nations that violet trade agreements and thereby harm American workers. To implement these strategies Trump is appointing the toughest and smartest people in the trade team to ensure that Americans have the best negotiators possible. [37]

Trump's *America First Energy Policy* has economic implications not only for America but also for other

---

[37] Whitehouse.gov, *Trade Deals that Work for all Americans,* retrieved on February 2, 2017 from https://www.whitehouse.gov/trade-deals-working-all-americans

nations especially the OPEC member nations. The Policy seeks to lower costs for Americans, maximize the use of American resources and free it from dependence on foreign oil. It will use shale oil and gas revolution to create jobs and bring prosperity to the nation, taking the advantage of an estimated $50 trillion in untapped shale, oil and gas natural resources. The Trump administration is committed to achieving energy independence from OPEC cartel and nations antagonistic to American interests but at the same working with its Gulf allies for developing positive energy relationship as part of an anti–terrorism strategy.[38]

Trump's Executive Orders reflecting his Protectionist Policies

On his first Monday in office, Trump signed an executive order for America to withdraw from the Trans-Pacific Partnership (TPP), which, as he argues, was harmful to American workers and the manufacturing industry. The TPP was negotiated during the regime President Barrack Obama and was never ratified by the Congress.[39]

---

[38] Whitehouse.gov *An America First Energy Plan* retrieved on February 2, 2017 from https://www.whitehouse.gov/america-first-energy

[39] Jeremy Diamond and Dana Bash (2017) "Trans-Pacific Partnership trade deal withdrawal Trump's first executive action" , *CNNPolitics.com*,

Twelve countries that border the Pacific Ocean signed up for the TPP in February 2016 to deepen economic ties between them, slash tariffs and foster trade to boost growth and promote a closer relationship on economic policies and regulations. All the 12 nations have to ratify it before it could come into effect. The countries are US, Japan, Malaysia, Vietnam, Singapore and Brunei. The rest are Australia, New Zealand, Canada, Mexico, Chile and Peru. The countries involved have a collective population of about 800 million that almost doubles that of the European Union's single market. The deal would have strengthen America's position in the Asia-Pacific region where China is growing in influence, but its opponents see it as a secretive deal that would favour big business and other countries to the detriment of American jobs and national sovereignty. The U.S. pulling out of the deal will be a big blow for the remaining nations.[40]

On January 23, 2017 Donald Trump signed an executive order to renegotiate the North American Free Trade Agreement (NAFTA) to get a better deal for American workers. NAFTA involves U.S. trade agreement with

---

retrieved on February 2, 2017 from https://edition.cnn.com/2017/23/politics/trans-pacific-parnership-trade-deal-withdrawal-first-executive-action-monday-sources-say/

[40] *TPP: What is it and why does it matter.* Retrieved on February 6, 2017 from http://www.bbc.com/news/business-32498715

Canada and Mexico. Trump threatened that his country will withdraw if other NAFTA members don't agree to renegotiate. This will mean reinstatement of tariffs on trade between United States, Canada and Mexico.[41]

NAFTA was created 20 years ago to promote trade between United States, Canada and Mexico and make the countries more competitive in the global market place. It benefits include boosting economic growth in all the three countries and lowering prices for gas and food for Americans. The negative impacts include reducing jobs in U.S. and sending them to Mexico, and exploiting Mexican farmers and the environment. Between 1994 and 2010, U.S. recorded $97.2 billion trade deficit with Mexico which displaced 682,900 U.S. jobs. States of California, New York, Michigan and Texas had high concentrations of manufacturing industries that moved their plants to Mexico.[42]

On January 25, 2017, Trump signed the executive order to build a wall along the 2000- mile border with Mexico at an estimated cost of $10 billon to $20 billion. On

---

[41] Amadeo, Kimberly, (2017) *Donal Trump and NAFTA,* retrieved on February 2, 2017 from https://www.thebalance.com/donald-trump-nafta-4111368

[42] Amadeo, Kimberly, (2017) *Do NAFTA's 6 Pros Outweigh its 6 Cons ?,* retrieved on February 2, 2017 from https://www.thebalance.com/nafta-pros-and-cons-3970481

January 27, 2017, another executive order (Executive Order 13769) to stop the U.S. refugee program for four months and ban the entry of citizens from Iran, Somalia, Sudan, Syria, Libya, Iraq and Yemen into America for 90 days, was signed. Following the court ban on this order, its second edition was signed by President Donald Trump on Monday 6th March 2017. The revised order bans citizens from six Muslim-majority nations from traveling to the United States but excludes Iraq from the former list containing seven Muslim nations. It still keeps a 90-day ban on travel to the United States by citizens of the remaining six nations. Iraq was removed from the list of the banned countries because its government has imposed new vetting procedures such as heightened visa screening and data sharing. It is also working with the U.S. in countering the so-called Islamic State militants. In addition, legal permanent residents in the United States, that is, the green card holders from the listed countries would not be affected by the new travel ban. March 16, 2017 was fixed as the effective date of the new order.[43]

---

[43] For details refer to Steve Holland and Julia Edwards Ainsley (2017) "President Trump signs new executive order on immigration, drops Iraq from travel ban," *AOL Inc*. Retrieved on March 7, 2017 from https://www.aol.com/article/news/2017/03/06/president-trump-signs-new-executive-order-on-immigration/21874502/ and also The White House (2017) *Executive Order Protecting The Nation From Foreign Terrorist Entry Into The United States*. Retrieved on March 7, 2017 from

Repercussions of the Trump's Protectionist Policies

Wharton International Management Professor, Mauro Guillen, says protectionism is a "terrible idea," and that "Every time you're introducing protectionism, you're hurting the consumer." In addition, there is also the issue of substitution, a 20% tariff on Mexican goods, for instance, will not necessarily lead people to automatically buy more products made in America. Some consumers and companies could go to China or Indonesia, or Costa Rica. On Trump's pledge to build a wall between the U.S. and Mexico to stem the flow of undocumented workers and somehow make Mexico pay for it, Kent Smetters, Wharton Professor of Business Economics and Public Policy and former Deputy Assistant Secretary for Economic Policy under President George W. Bush, argues that deporting these workers — estimated between 11 million and 12 million overall — would harm the U.S. economy. The assumption that if these workers were deported, native-born workers would take over these jobs is not empirically true.[44]

---

https://www.whitehouse.gov/the-press-office/2017/03/06/executive-order-protecting-nation-foreign-terrorist-entry-united-states

[44] For details, see Wharton School of the University of Pennsylvania (2017) *How Will Trump's Policies Affect the U.S. Economy?* Retrieved on February 6, 2017 from

Six weeks to the swearing-in of Trump, the Economics Editor of the Guardian, Larry Elliott, had written an article on the implications of Donald Trump's victory in the U.S. presidential elections for the global economy. Starting with Mexico, America's neighbour, Elliot states that Trump has threatened to put a 35% tariff on some Mexican goods, close the "sweatshops in Mexico that undercut American workers" and send home about 5 million illegal immigrants living and working in America. Implementing these in full would slow trade between the U.S. and Mexico, close factories and dry up foreign direct investment flows while U.S. consumers would experience rises in the price of some goods. As for China, the U.S. is the largest single market for Chinese exports, accounting for about 20% of the total. Imposing a 45% tariff on its goods coming into the U.S. to enable American companies to compete with it could result in a marked slowdown in China's growth and a loss of manufacturing jobs. If these happen, China would have the option of promising to increase direct investment in America in support of Trump's attempt to rebuild the American Economy or

---

http://knowledge.wharton.upenn.edu/article/trumps-policies-economy-wharton-experts-weigh/

adopt an aggressive, nationalistic stance. The repercussion of America possibly leaving the Trans-Pacific Partnership, which President Barrack Obama regarded as way of keeping countries such as Japan, Brunei, Singapore and Malaysia out of China's control, and which have an export–led model of growth, would be slower growth across Asia as there are signs that countries such as South Korea and Taiwan will be subjected to the same protectionist restrictions as Mexico and China. Like Asia, the euro zone is heavily reliant on exports as a source of growth. A more restrictive U.S. trade regime will affect the zone. The UK will not be immune from any slowdown in the global economy that might result from a Trump victory even though it is the second biggest exporter of services in the world with America being the largest importer of them. As Trump's protectionist measures centre on cheap manufactured goods, rather than the high-end services which Britain provides, there seems to be little reason to fear that any new barriers will be created by the Trump administration for UK firms.[45]

Despite the fact that Trump's proposed actions can be seen to add value to the American manufacturing sector, the trading partners in Asia and Latin America

---

[45] Larry Elliott (2016) "How America's new president will affect the global economy" Retrieved on February 8, 2017 from
https://www.theguardian.com/business/2016/nov/09/donald-trump-new-us-president-america-global-economy-china-mexico

may liken them to economic decline. Attempts to reduce the U.S. trade deficit under Trump's policies will likely benefit U.S. workers and strengthen GDP growth at least in the short term but the long term repercussions of a dramatic policy shift to economic independence from one of globalization are debatable. Finally, the process of renegotiating existing trade agreements, in addition to the enforcement of international law upon economic superpowers such as China, will create many unique challenges.[46]

Desmond Lachman, Resident Fellow at the American Enterprise Institute, a former a Deputy Director in the International Monetary Fund's Policy Development and Review Department and also the Chief Emerging Market Economic Strategist at Salomon Smith Barney, observes that Donald Trump seems to be ignoring how the very integrated the U.S. economic and financial system is with the rest of the world. This raises the real risk that his economic policies could destabilize the global economy and negatively affect the U.S. economic recovery. In addition, Trump's disregard for the multilateral lending institutions and his strong skepticism about the need for continued U.S.

---

[46] For details refer to the article *How Will President Trump's Policies Affect Trade and Economics?* Retrieved on February 6, 2017 from https://www.fxcm.com/insights/how-will-president-trumps-policies-affect-trade-and-economics/

international economic leadership could be highly problematic for the world economy in the event of the bursting of the global credit bubble created through years of highly unorthodox monetary policies. He adds, "Among the more immediate global economic challenges likely to confront Trump will be China, the world's second largest economy and until recently the major source of global economic growth." There are very clear signs that that China's credit bubble is beginning to burst, its capital outflow problem is again gaining momentum. Trump keeps branding China as a currency manipulator, cheapening its currency despite the fact that over the past year it has burnt through over $1 trillion in its international reserves in order to prevent the excessive weakening of its currency.[47]

Reactions to the Trump's Protectionist Policies

Geoffrey Garrett, a Wharton dean, hopes that "the protectionist impulses of the Trump administration stay more in the realm of rhetoric than reality, symbols rather than tariffs." He argues that free trade improves the living standards of people because it lowers the cost of goods and services and produces economic

---

[47] For more details see Desmond Lachman, (2017) *"Trump's economic policies could destabilize the global economy" The Hill* January 6, 2017. Retrieved of February 7, 2017 from http://thehill.com/blogs/pundits-blog/finance/312980-how-trumps-economic-policies-could-destabilize-the-global-economy

winners and losers, and that compensating the losers, being few, concentrated workers that lost their jobs to foreigners, can be away of offsetting its negative effects. He further argues that rapid technological change coupled with economic stagnation in Middle America had caused more pain than free trade. So the biggest challenges for the Trump administration are increasing America's growth rate and helping more Americans to benefit from the revolution in information technology.[48]

Chad P. Bown, Senior Fellow at the Peterson Institute for International Economics in Washington, says the claims by Trump and other U.S. politicians that the destination-based cash flow tax (DBCFT) is designed to discriminate against Mexico or any other trading partner, would in the best-case scenario, bring trade dispute. The DBCFT replaces the current corporate income tax. He adds that the formal dispute settlement system is the most under-appreciated part of today's trade agreements which are designed to depoliticize trade issues. Working outside of the trade agreement

---

[48] For details, see Wharton School of the University of Pennsylvania (2017) *Do Trade Agreements Lead to Income Inequality?* Retrieved on February 6, 2017 from http://knowledge.wharton.upenn.edu/article/do-trade-agreements-lead-to-income-inequality/

system would lead to retaliation and counter–retaliation, a self-defeating trade war could erupt, and just like what happened in the 1930s, this could have destructive implications for all the economies involved. He further declares that there is "is little to gain and much to lose by motivating a border tax adjustment as either a punitive import tariff or a policy designed to finance the construction of a border wall."[49]

Emily Stewart submits that certainly, Trump has some grandiose ideas and a lofty rhetoric to accompany them but understanding the exact nature of his economic policies is a complex task. Trump initially focused his attention on immigration reform, calling for a wall to be built between Mexico and the United States and demanding the deportation of 11 million undocumented immigrants. His plans cost him a handful of business deals, but they might cost the United States much more. Citing the American Action Forum, a right–leaning policy institute based in Washington D.C., Stewart writes that the Forum has estimated that enforcing current immigration law fully and immediately, as Trump has recommended, would cost the federal

---

[49] Chad Bown (2017) *"Trump's border tax is not the right fix for U.S.-Mexico trade" PBS Newshour,* January 30, 2017. Retrieved on February 6, 2017 from http://www.pbs.org/newshour/making-sense/column-trumps-border-tax-not-right-fix-u-s-mexico-trade/

government from $400 billion to $600 billion. The labour force would fall by 11 million workers, the real GDP would be reduced by $1.6 trillion and that would take 20 years to complete. Doug Holtz-Eakin, president of the Forum and the chief economic policy adviser to Sen. John McCain's 2008 presidential campaign, says doing this "will harm the U.S. economy" and also perceives immigration as "an enormous source of economic vitality." [50]

Reactions to President Donald Trump's executive order stopping the U.S. refugee program for four months and banning the entry of citizens from seven predominantly Muslim countries into America for 90 days, included protests by thousands of people that gathered at airports across the country to express their support for travelers from those countries who were being detained.

The order, according to experts, could undermine the reputation of the U.S. as a reliable place to do business. Experts at Wharton and Howard University, for instance, discussed the longer–term implications of the travel ban on the *Knowledge@Wharton* show on

---

[50] Emily Stewart (2017) "With Donald Trump as President, Here's What Will Happen to the U.S. Economy" *The Street* Jan 29, 2017. Retrieved on February 7, 2017 from https://www.thestreet.com/story/13335121/1/if-donald-trump-was-president-here-s-what-would-happen-to-the-u-s-economy.html

Wharton Business Radio on SiriusXM channel 111. They included Michael Useem, Wharton management professor and director of the Center for Leadership and Change Management. He said the U.S. growth rate was suffering, and its companies "need great people. Where do they come from? Pretty much everywhere." "We want stability in our markets, and people and goods moving across borders without arbitrary restrictions...," he added. He also pointed to a statement by Mark Zuckerberg, the Facebook CEO, that everybody benefits "when the best and brightest from around the world can live, work and contribute here." Ronil Hira, a political science professor at Howard University, also spoke during the discussion programme, pointing out that Trump's action was not aimed specifically at H-1B visas or workers in the tech industry, it was meant to fulfill a commitment made to supporters during his campaign and was a broader issue of national security. Another discussant, Robert Meyer, Wharton marketing professor and co-director of the Risk Management and Decision Processes Center, pointed out that the U.S. image as the world leader in higher education was also under threat while several universities had shown concerns on the impact on faculty and students from the seven countries affected by the ban.[51]

---

[51] For details, see Wharton School of the University of Pennsylvania (2017) *How the Immigration Ban Will Impact U.S. Businesses*, retrieved on February 6, 2017 from

Reactions in support and in condemnation of Trump's decision to halt all refugee admissions and temporarily bar people from the seven Muslim nations were also expressed by international organizations, world leaders and other notable personalities. Here are some of the reactions which were reported by the BBC:[52]

1. The United Nations called on Mr Trump to continue protecting refugees, regardless of race, nationality or religion.

2. The Arab League, which has 22 member states including most of the countries directly affected by the ban, expressed deep concern about the "unjustified restrictions".

3. Amnesty International called the order an "appalling move with potentially catastrophic consequences".

4. Human Rights Watch said the order was a "blow" to refugees, and that it would "do little to

---

http://knowledge.wharton.upenn.edu/article/trumps-policies-economy-wharton-experts-weigh/

[52] "Trump executive order banning refugees: World reacts," BBC, January 29, 2017. http://www.bbc.com/news/world-us-canada-38781973 Accessed on February 8, 2017.

address terrorism and other national security threats".

5. The American Immigration Lawyers Association said: "Broad language in the order appears to be designed to target people of Muslim faith."

6. UK Prime Minister, Theresa May, said she does "not agree" with the ban, and will intervene if it affects British citizens.

7. Canada's Prime Minister, Justin Trudeau, tweeted: "To those fleeing persecution, terror and war, Canadians will welcome you, regardless of your faith. Diversity is our strength."

8. German leader, Angela Merkel, believes it is not justified to put people from a specific background or faith under general suspicion, according to her spokesperson.

9. Mayor of London, Sadiq Khan, said "President Trump's ban on refugees and immigrants from certain countries is shameful and cruel."

10. French President, François Hollande, warned that a protectionist approach would be a "dead end".

11. President of the Czech Republic, Milos Zeman, praised Mr Trump's order. His spokesman said on Twitter: "US President Trump protects his country, he's concerned with the safety of his citizens. Exactly what EU elites do not do".

12. Dutch anti-Islam political leader, Geert Wilders, tweeted: "Well done @POTUS it's the only way to stay safe + free. I would do the same. Hope you'll add more Islamic countries like Saudi Arabia soon".

There were also reactions to the immigration ban from the business community in America, especially from the owners of information technology–related enterprises. In an article posted by a group of writers and published by TechCrunch, reactions from several executives of firms in the U.S. information technology industry have shown their displeasure with Trump's executive order which temporarily halted the admission of refugees, indefinitely banned the admission of refugees from Syria, and stopped citizens of seven Muslim-majority countries from entering the U.S.

As reported in the article, Google had already recalled its employees from abroad and wrote in an official statement "We're concerned about the impact of this order and any proposals that could impose restrictions on Googlers and their families, or that create barriers to bringing great talent to the U.S. ." Facebook founder and CEO, Mark Zuckerberg noted in a Facebook post that he was "concerned about the impact of the recent executive orders signed by President Trump," while Twitter CEO, Jack Dorsey, criticized the executive order. The Microsoft CEO, Satya Nadella, said in a post on LinkedIn, "As an immigrant and as a CEO, I've both experienced and seen the positive impact that immigration has on our company, for the country, and for the world. We will continue to advocate on this important topic." Noting that many Fortune 500 companies are founded by immigrants or their children, the LinkedIn CEO, Jeff Weiner, wrote "All ethnicities should have access to opportunity — founding principle of U.S." Uber CEO, Travis Kalanick, in an email to his team said that the order affected about "a dozen or so employees." Adobe CEO, Shantanu Narayen, also in a message to all employees of the company, said "as an immigrant, US citizen and CEO, I am deeply concerned about the impact of the recent executive order restricting entry into the United States for nationals of seven countries, and I know many of you are as well." Twilio CEO, Jeff Lawson, calls the ban "fundamentally UnAmerican" while Mozilla CEO, Chris Beard, said that he believed that "The immigration ban imposed by Friday's executive order is overly broad and its implementation is highly disruptive to fostering a culture of innovation and economic growth." Red Hat gave the following as part of its statement: "Red Hat is strong because of the thousands of diverse voices that comprise our company. Our continued work to advance the technology industry depends greatly on our ability to attract the best and brightest talent from around the world." Pinterest CEO, Ben Silbermann, gave the following statement to TechCrunch: "Inclusivity makes our company stronger, and the same is true for this country. We oppose this ban which affects many innocent people." Part of an email sent to all staff from Amazon's vice president of HR, Beth Galetti, reads "Amazon has been committed to equal rights, tolerance and diversity—and we always will be. As we've grown the company, we've worked hard to attract talented people from all over the world, and we believe this is one of the things that make Amazon great."[53]

The several protests rallies and marches that took place in American cities and other cities around the globe also formed part of reactions to Trump's Executive Order on Immigration. Some of these reactions also need to be stated as examples of what had happened. Demonstrations against the executive order were held

---

[53] To see all the reactions, refer to Frederick Lardinois, Kate Conger, Mathew Linly and Darrell Hethering (2017) "Tech Reacts to Trump's Immigration Ban," Techcrunch, January 28, 2017. Retrieved from https://techcrunch.com/2017/01/28/tech-companies-react-to-immigration-ban/

in cities across America on Sunday January 28, 2017. Several protesters were seen at airports opposing the order which they perceived as un-American. In Washington, thousands of protesters gathered outside the front lawn of the White House to show their anger with Trump's decision and their solidarity with Muslims. They chanted "Shame," and later "No hate, no fear". Boos and profanities rented the air while marchers passed the Trump International Hotel in Washington. Thousands of other protesters attended a rally at Battery Park in Lower Manhattan. Through tears, Asma Shu'aib, a student, renounced violence in the name of Islam and said she joined the protest to resist Trump's order. Lawyers at the international arrival terminal of San Francisco International Airport, like their counter parts in other parts of America, were holding up signs of offers for free assistance to people awaiting the arrival of family members coming from the seven countries affected by the order. Thousands of protesters accompanied by brass band and drummers were chanting "Say it loud, say it clear, refugees are welcome here!"[54]

On February 12, 2017 about 20,000 people marched through the capital city of Mexico demanding respect

---

[54] "Demonstrators in Streets, and at Airports, Protest Immigration Order" New York Times, January 29, 2017. Accessed on February 9, 2017 from https://mobile.nytimes.com/2017/01/29/us/protests-airports-donald-trump-immigration-executive-ordrer-muslims.html

for their country and its citizens in the US facing perceived hostility from the Trump's administration, and protesting against Trump's plan for a boarder wall and deportation of migrants. Many of them carried Mexican flags. Some carried banners and placards with different inscriptions, Paulina Arteaga's placard, for instance, reads: "We love Americans, we hate racism." A university Professor, Irene Aguilar, said the main message of the marchers was to show the unity of Mexicans in times of hardship.[55]

Litigations were also part of the reactions to Trump's Executive Order on Immigration. The states of Washington and Minnesota won the court case which led to the putting the ban of immigration on hold. They argued that re-introduction of the ban by the Federal Appeals court would bring chaos again. But Justice Department lawyers, countered, saying citizens outside the United States had "no substantive right or basis for judicial review in the denial of visas at all." 10 high-ranking diplomatic and national security officials, 100 Silicon Valley tech companies, 280 law professors and 16 state or district attorneys general and civil liberties

---

[55] "Thousands March in Mexico to Demand Respect, Reject Trump." VOA News February 13, 2017, retrieved on February 13, 2017 from https://www.voanews.com/a/thousands-march- in- mexico- to- demand – respect-and-reject- trump /3720396.html

organization formally expressed their support for the legal action against Trump's order.[56]

Instead of going to the Supreme Court to challenge the ruling by an Appeals Court, President Trump signed a revised executive order on immigration on March 6, 2017, but in less than a week it was challenged by six states. The state of Hawaii is the first to file a suit, arguing that the new order will harm Muslims living in the Pacific island state. Five other states, namely, Washington, Oregon, Minnesota, Massachusetts and New York banded together in a combined challenge to the revised order. Bob Ferguson, Washington state's attorney general, said the states have a solid legal argument and that the new order is "narrower" than the old version but "that does not mean that it's cured its constitutional problems."[57]

---

[56] Matt Zapotosky (2017) "Federal Appeals Court Decides to Schedule a Hearing on Trump Travel Order" *The Washington Post*, February 6, 2017. Retrieved on February 8 from https://www.washingtonpost.com/world/national-security/opposition-to-trump-travel-ban-grows-as-key-court-decision-looms/2017/02/06/d766ec7c-ec74-11e6-9662-6eedf1627882_story.html?utm_term=.7b9041f0d0d5

[57] Ken Schwart (2017) *6 U.S. States Challenge Trump's Revised Travel Ban*. Retrieved on March 11, 2017 from http://www.voanews.com/a/four-us-states-challenge-donald-trump-travel-ban/3757550.html

The revised travel ban was also put on hold on Wednesday, March 16 2017 by Derrick Watson, a U.S. District Court Judge in Hawaii, just hours before it was to come into effect. The judgment was in response to a lawsuit filed by Hawii State alleging that the new ban was essentially a Muslim ban and it will hurt state businesses, damage tourism industry and stop universities from recruiting top talent. On the following day, another federal judge in Maryland issued a second, but narrower injunction – suspending only part of the order which stopped the issuance of visa to citizens of the affected Muslim nations. During a rally in Nashville, Tennessee, President Trump reacted to the Hawii court order, calling it "terrible" and vowed to fight it up to the Supreme Court. The Department of Justice also strongly disagreed with the ruling.[58]

Lessons from the American Experience

The lessons one can draw from the experiences Americans and other people have with the Trump's protectionist policies in the era of advanced

---

[58] Matt Zapotosky, Kalani Takase and Maria Sacchetti and (2017) *"Federal judge in Hawaii freezes President Trump's new entry ban"* The *Washington Post* , March 16, 2017. Retrieved on March 16, 2017 from https://www.washingtonpost.com/local/social-issues/lawyers-face-off-on-trump-travel-ban-in-md-court-wednesday-morning/2017/03/14/

globalization are many. The prominent ones include the following:

a) Majority of the reactions from world leaders, international organizations, business owners and Americans that took part in protests and marches were not in support of the protectionist policies introduced by the Trump's administration. Here, the lesson for the entire world is that protectionism in unpopular in the present day.

b) The expressed disapproval of the protectionist policies come people that cut across faiths, race, nationality and socio-economic status. This means there is a general disapproval for protectionist policies in America.

c) Many non-Muslims were not in support of the executive order banning the entry of citizens from seven predominantly Muslim countries into America. In fact, they even express their solidarity with the Muslims. Thus instead of creating a division between people belonging to different faiths, the order further united them.

d) Economists and business owners have perceived protectionism as an evil that will bring negative repercussions not only to businesses and the American economy, but also to the global economy. This means there are prospects for people to embrace globalism especially when they understand its advantages over protectionism and the pursuit of narrow national interests.

e) Another lesson from the reactions and arguments expressed by experts and scholars is that there is a general fear that the protectionist policies in U.S will harm its economy as well as the global economy.

CHAPTER FIVE

THE TWELVE FACTS

Introduction

This chapter identifies the twelve facts which serve as the main conclusions from the discourse on protectionism and the global economy. Based on the premise that globalization is irreversible and unavoidable; the chapter also provides recommendations on how businesses and nations can cope and live with the forces of globalization.

The Twelve Facts

The twelve facts about protectionism and the global economy summarize and reflect the contents of the previous chapters of this book. They are as follows:

1. Economic thought is dynamic. It changes with prevailing challenges and circumstances. Protectionism, being an essential component of mercantilism, does not suit the present era of advanced globalization.

2. The physiocrats' criticism of mercantilism, more specifically, their argument that the hope of obtaining national gains at the cost of other countries is an illusion, is still valid. This is because the downside of economic policies that

are harmful to other nations can offset their benefits.

3. Protectionism is an important element of mercantilism. It is manifested by regulation of a nation's economy for the purpose of augmenting state power at the expense of rival nations, imposing high tariffs on the importation of finished goods to protect the interest of local manufacturers, restraining imports and encouraging exports. Other aspects of protectionism are the banning the export of tools and capital equipment and the emigration of skilled labour to other nations with view to discouraging them from competing with firms producing goods and services in the country implementing mercantilist policies.

4. David Ricardo's theory of comparative advantage, that is, there would be gains from trade if each nation specializes in the production of the commodity in which it has a comparative cost advantage in producing and then buys the other commodity from the other nation, is also still valid. Instead of each country committing its resources to the production of everything in pursuit of illusive and unrealistic self- reliance, it should devout its resources to what it can do better with the available endowments, productive capacity and expertise. It should meet other needs through trade with other

nations. This will promote global peace and cooperation among nations.

5. From the arguments in support of mercantilism as well as criticisms against it, it is true that the disadvantages of protectionism, especially with the advancement in globalization, outweigh its benefits. Protectionism is largely harmful to the global economy by restricting competition in production of goods and services, and reducing consumer satisfaction and standard of living. Protectionism can also spur misunderstanding and fan the embers of hatred among members of the international community.

6. Every nation has interests similar to the interests of other nations but the strategies, wherewithal and commitment for its realization could differ. Moreover, every nation has its own peculiarities and priorities. National interests, more often than not, cover desire for economic prosperity and social security, protection of citizens, animals and the environment in general, facilitation of educational and spiritual development of people, ensuring people's access to healthcare services, protection of freedom and human rights, etc. Each of these aspects of national interests can translate into policies and strategies for their meaningful realization.

7. Interests of nations running the global economy would naturally and inevitably clash, just as the interest of the buyer of a commodity aiming for a low price clashes with that of its seller aiming for a high price. This clash does not preclude the transaction; in addition, it does not render the contending parties enemies. They are simply business partners agreeing to settle their differences according to the rules of the game. The same principle should apply to the pursuit of national interest based on treaties, international laws and trade agreements.

8. The global economy will prosper when world leaders and policy makers prefer positive globalism to nationalism. Nationalism, which has been defined 'a feeling of love for and pride in your country; a feeling that your country is better than any other,' could encourage world leaders and policy makers to have little or no concern for the development and wellbeing of people of other countries.[59] The world will become more united in confronting the problems of poverty, illiteracy, malnutrition, global warming, terror and violation of human and animal rights if world leaders accept positive globalism which means showing love and concern for humanity in general and taking legitimate measures to promote its wellbeing

---

[59] These definitions are given by the *Oxford Advanced Learner's Dictionary* (2007 edition) Oxford: Oxford University Press.

without discriminations based on race, culture and geographical location. Negative globalism means surrendering the sovereignty of individual nations to an amalgam of a dictatorial authority or organization seeking to dominate them through biased laws and regulations, evil plotting and machinations. This is objectionable.

9. Immigration is an important factor in the design and implementation of protectionist policies, it is also important to the development of the global economy. This is because tapping cheaper foreign labour markets and free transfer of services across national frontiers invariably involves movement of people across national frontiers. As the possession of talent is not the preserve of a particular people from a particular race, culture, belief or geographical location, the benefits that the global economy stands to gain from immigration is enormous. This explains why the American experience with the recent protectionist immigration policies met unprecedented rejection from people of diverse cultures, faiths and nationalities.

10. Globalization is not new thing, its development as the result of advancement in information and communication technology and the resultant effect of this development on the global economy and the economies of individual nations are what make it more noticeable in the 21st century. Globalization will never cease to

exist and it will continue to influence economies of the world in both positive and negative ways because at any point in time, when two parties transact a business, at least one partly will benefit from it, and as one door closes, another one opens. Forcing people to have a uniform culture, way of life and belief is the aspect of globalization that is counter to reality and God's design. Diversity in these areas will never cease to exist. If put to good use, this diversity provides business opportunities and a means of identifying people and the communities to which they belong. It is also a means of testing one's ability to treat, relate and interact with human beings with objectivity, fairness and justice. Cultural diversity makes the world an interesting place to live in. People save money to travel to places and observe different cultures.

11. The global economy is increasingly becoming integrated and inter dependent. It is characterized by complex interactions between national economies and the global economy, and by complex combinations of national economies with regional economies, transnational economic actors and international institutions.

12. With the ever increasing forces of globalization, achieving macroeconomic policy objectives by any single nation is becoming increasingly ineffective. Nations have to sit together to

fashion out mutually beneficial globoeconomic policies that will also promote peace and understanding among them. These features make it basically incompatible with protectionism.

Recommendations

The following recommendations are made based on some of the facts about the relationship between protectionism and the global economy:

   a) Immigration as an important factor in the design and implementation of protectionist policies and in the development of the global economy needs to be handled with great care to avoid the kind of reactions seen in the United States in the wave of the President Trump's immigration policies. Leaders and politicians must shun inflammatory speeches which fan the embers of xenophobia among their followers.

   b) The general populace needs to be educated about protectionism, globalization, positive globalism and the global economy as well as their import and implications to their lives, the economies of their countries of origin and the entire world. This work can be done by governments, development partners, individuals and non-governmental organizations.

c) Since globalization will never cease to exist and it will continue to influence economies of the world in both positive and negative ways, nations need to learn to live and cope with it like a diabetic needing to learn to live with his / her health problems in the absence of pills that can wipe them out completely.

d) As the aspect of globalization seeking to make people uniform in culture and belief, runs counter to reality and God's will, people need to respect diversity and tolerate one another. What a person from a given cultural background cherishes will never be the same with what other persons from other cultural backgrounds would cherish.

www.ingramcontent.com/pod-product-compliance
Lightning Source LLC
Chambersburg PA
CBHW070106210526
45170CB00013B/772